Natasha Maingi

Microsoft Business Information Systems

GRIN Publishing

Bibliographic information published by the German National Library:

The German National Library lists this publication in the National Bibliography; detailed bibliographic data are available on the Internet at http://dnb.dnb.de .

Imprint:

Print and binding: Books on Demand GmbH, Norderstedt Germany
ISBN: 978-3-656-60117-3

This book at GRIN:

http://www.grin.com/en/e-book/269108/microsoft-business-information-systems

Table of Contents

Evaluation of Business Information System at Microsoft

Information is necessary for many businesses whether small, medium, or large, and the necessity of the information depends on a variety of uses. For example, in the case of proper planning in the business, senior managers will require information to facilitate this planning. However, middle-level management relies on detailed systems of information in order to properly control and monitor various activities in the business. At the same time, various employees who have operational roles also tend to rely on information systems in order to efficiently carry out their duties in the business. Due to all these necessities, many businesses tend to develop information systems that operate at the same time. The Microsoft Company applies Management Information Systems (MIS) in dealing with internal affairs of the company. An Office Automation System (OAS) improves the productivity of employees who need to process data and information (Bill 2006). The Microsoft Company deals with several software systems and the use of OAS becomes handy since it enhances employees' productivity. Employees have the ability to work from their own homes, as well as other areas at their convenience. Apart from these two systems of information, the other systems of information applicable by the Microsoft Company is the use of Decision Support Systems commonly known as DSS. A decision support system enables the management to make decisions in situations surrounded by uncertainty (Bill 2006). A lot of uncertainty occasionally arises from these big companies such as Microsoft and in such times, the use of DSS becomes handy. This method consists of techniques and tools capable of collecting relevant information and providing analysis of all the relevant information gathered. In the process of analysis provisions, the method also provides alternatives used in case of absence of relevant information. Apart from the provisions of alternatives, this method also involves the use of complex spreadsheets and various databases used to develop several "what-if" models.

Critical Analysis of MIS, DSS, and OAS Information Systems

With a relational database such as an SQL Server, the Microsoft Company uses MIS to develop Custom Information Systems (CIS). The development of custom information systems enables data linking during its entry, which thus enables cross-referencing with various reports and finally turns the information into valuable and useful information. Collection and analysis of information is possible with a well-developed data model, and the well-developed data model enables the company to understand their clients as well as being in a state to predict and tell market trends and future sales of the company (Bill 2006). Tailoring of software to the exact requirements of the company is possible, and the company is also capable of using and providing in-depth administrative reports and charts them. The Microsoft Company also uses MIS to link various existing database software as Sage and MySQL in order to create various comprehensive reports. The company can also use MIS to carry out questionnaire analysis using Access software, together with Microsoft Word and Excel (Bill 2006). The staffs at Microsoft are also capable of easily managing all completed process of questionnaire creation through logging contacts with respondents, as well as exporting and importing reports within the questionnaire.

Various other companies in need of custom Contact Management software uses this software to market their various products, and in such situations, Microsoft becomes handy in the integration of their databases. During such cases, the Microsoft Company uses MIS to automate various regulatory processes for these companies. When managing the expansion of services in these companies, the companies use Microsoft Access databases integrated with Excel and Word in order to facilitate the expansion. In order to facilitate this process, the company automates its software using MIS.

Critical Analysis of DSS

When writing applications, the use of services becomes helpful when designing building blocks and services are easy to use with DSS. The Microsoft Company uses DSS when developing Service Tutorials Overview and these tutorials help in the demonstration of various concepts and terminologies applicable by this company. The company uses DSS to represent Hardware components; for example, the actuators, the sensors, software components like storage, directory and User Interface, as well as for aggregations purposes. Execution of services takes place in the context of the DSS node and the company uses a DSS as a hosting environment. The various services awaiting creation and management are under support from the DSS node and hosting lasts until the services are either deleted or stopped. Microsoft carries out networking of services using DSS for easy communication in a uniform manner. The company is capable of reusing their services through the use of DSS, and this is because of the feature that enables it to describe a set of components within a given section (Bill 2006). The company is capable of assigning a Universal Resource Identifier (URI) using the constructor service, and it is capable of running in the DSS node.

The company carries out their services communication using DSS Accessing Services and this possible by linking to the Web Browser.

Critical Analysis of Office Automation Systems

Streamlining of work flow within software produced by the Microsoft Company is achievable using office automation systems. Through these systems, the company is capable of building custom applications capable of tracking and typing all the information required by the company. Using automation systems, Microsoft is capable of creating worksheets which were later used to develop Excel programs, as well as to read information and databases. Automation also enables the company to create software capable of validating other software before the user saves them. Microsoft was capable of creating an Outlook program with the ability to send custom forms to individuals or groups, at the same time saving information in Excel spreadsheets and several databases.

How Microsoft can use these Systems for Competitive / Strategic Value

The company can apply the above information systems to come up with new software that will surpass other software provided by other rival companies like Android and Mac OS. The use of Android is slowly becoming popular with mobile industries.

Porter's 5 Forces Model

There are five major crucial forces that determine the competitiveness of any given organization according to the five forces analysis; the supplier power is one of the suggested forces. Microsoft has easily managed to deliver its prices to their suppliers. This was as the result of the drive number of supplies to each key input. The non-comparison of the products and services that Microsoft offers to their clients has given them the strength and an added advantage to have control over their competitors. The products include the operating system; Windows 7 Enterprise. This is one of the products that have dominated a vast market all around the world. The services have also allowed them to remain on the frontline, for instance the direct access which gives millions of users' seamless access to corporate networks without the need of VPN. There, many other services that the company offers are perceived as a monopoly in the market. This fact has enabled Microsoft to have fewer supplier choices and hence, more need for suppliers' help; the result is that their suppliers have gained a lot of power. This strategy has ensured that Microsoft's prices remain relatively high as determined by their suppliers (El Shazly & Butts 2002).

Buyer power is another core strategy tool recommended by Porter's five analysis model. This tool looks at how buyers have the power to drive the prices of the company's products down. Microsoft has ensured that it is well-established in many consumers. This is through numerous advertisements which the company has conducted around the world. As a result, Microsoft has gained several powerful consumers who purchase their products and services. The customers available to Microsoft from different regions give the added advantage on price control. Consumers can hardly gang up or form an alliance with an aim of controlling prices as it may be in the case of few consumers. This fact safeguards Microsoft in case one area consumers boycott their products and services since other consumers around the world will still purchase their products. Despite the fact that the customer is the most important person in any business enterprise, he or she should not have control over prices. The control the Microsoft Company has on buyer power has given it an advantage over its competitors.

Competition and rivalry are aspects which are well-observed by Microsoft. The company, since it was founded, has gained tremendous power year in and year out due to little competition (El Shazly & Butts 2002). The Microsoft Company has produced unique products and services; the lack of companies that produce similar products is the main reason behind this advantage. According to statistics, there is no other company that has proven to perform better compared to Microsoft. The products and services that Microsoft offers in the market have proven to be unique among consumers and hence, the demand has been maintained high throughout the market life. The lack of potential competitor has allowed Microsoft to remain the leading company among its competitors.

The threat of substitution is another crucial aspect covered by Porter's five forces analysis. The company has maintained the production of unique products which cannot easily be replaced by the consumer, and he or she still remains on the same level of utility satisfaction or goes on a higher indifference curve. The products and services from the company have high satisfaction among consumer satisfaction; no other product produced by any other company has been able to replace the products offered by Microsoft in the market. This fact has constrained consumers to highly rely on Microsoft's products since they only have few options. The company has made unique improvements on their products and this fact has allowed customers to achieve high satisfaction and remain loyal to the Microsoft Company (El Shazly & Butts 2002).

Microsoft has maintained its market power through the constant encounter of threats of new entries into the market. The Microsoft Company remains the leading company among its competitors and consumers due to its highly innovative technologies. The company has produced unique products which offer higher utility satisfaction among their consumers which has made the consumers remain loyal to Microsoft. This fact has made it hard for competitors to find a ready market for their products if they desire to invest in the same sector as Microsoft. Microsoft also has the advantage due to the high initial capital required by new investors in order to establish businesses similar to the company. Due to this aspect, Microsoft has maintained a favorable position over its competitors (El Shazly & Butts 2002)

Legal and Ethical Issues

Globally, Microsoft is among the most ethical firms due to the few ethical problems that arise from their operations. In fact, the company was listed among the most ethical companies in the world. However, some may question this rating because Microsoft has had its fair share of ethical issues. One of the ethical issues that Microsoft as an organization has faced is concerns about the security of its software. A breach in security software can lead to devastating consequences including huge losses by the client. In reference to this fact, Microsoft failed to achieve security of its software and as a result, unfortunate malicious programs were reported in its software. This can be attributed to the errors that existed in its operating system and some of its programs.

Another ethical issue that Microsoft faced was noncompliance with the standards that are set for use of its software. It is essential that an organization complies with certain standards that are set for its operation. A failure in this means failure to be ethical. As a result, this disadvantages other organizations operating in the same area of business. Microsoft was accused of locking out some of its customers, thus failing to adhere to the standards that guide the fair treatment of customers.

On many occasions, Microsoft has been accused of dealing in misleading advertisements. In an effort to attract more customers than its competitors, Microsoft has ended up advertising features that in its products that do not usually exist. The ‘free bundles’ it claims to provide if one purchases some of its products are not in the actual sense ‘free’. It does this to give the impression that it is aiding its customers while in reality, it is not. This allows consumers to make a choice based on misleading information.

The company has been involved in some legal battles that mainly arise due to copyright infringement (El Shazly & Butts 2002). Microsoft has been known to form alliances with some companies so as to enhance its network. However, there is a hidden agenda in these partnerships. The agenda is to have an assurance on loyalty that comes with these organizations. An infringement of copyright may therefore come about when Microsoft forces these companies to maintain their loyalty.

Another legal issue Microsoft has been involved in is where the company has been accused of trying to attain monopoly illegally. In order to achieve this, Microsoft is accused to have engaged in illegal activities so as to gain an advantage over its competitors. These activities entail critical evaluation of the strengths of its competitors and finding ways to gain an advantage over them. Identifying and capitalizing on their competitors' weaknesses is yet another way it has tried to gain an advantage over competitors. This is done to increase its profits. An increase in profits means that it will have more resources and as a result, enjoy economies of scale leading to the attainment of monopoly.

In an attempt to maintain its image, Microsoft has on several occasions gone to court to defend itself. It has not only tried to convince the judiciary about its innocence, but also the public. In its defense, Microsoft has tried to explain that it engages in legal activities and acts fairly in its quest to be the best software provider. In addition, it only engages in the innovation of its products.

Microsoft needs to contend with ethical and legal issues that accuse it of acting unfairly in order to attain monopoly. Whether this is true or not, it can be used by its competitors in order to discredit the company. A struggle in its part to prove the contrary is essential because losing this case means that Microsoft would experience huge losses. The effects would also spill over to the Microsoft management as the lawsuit would act as a distraction and prevent them from functioning optimally. This means that their productivity would diminish, further contributing to the company's losses.

Supply Chain Management Systems

The Supply Chain Management (SCM) automation at Microsoft reduces redundant tasks by increasing accuracy in the office and the customer receiving dock. It eliminates bottlenecks, improves order process, and minimizes the time of handling, thus promoting the efficiency of their operations (Nettleton & Jensen 2007). SCM also helps in the automation of information flow at Microsoft and assists the managers to make better decisions. The company also uses SCR to reduce uncertainty that arises because of inaccurate information, as well as to reduce the bullwhip effect. Since the implementation of SCR, Microsoft is in a position to accurately time orders as well as correctly place orders. The company has made it possible in reducing stock levels while expediting deliveries to their numerous customers. SCR software contains other software like supply chain planning software capable of carrying out supply chain execution. Through this software, Microsoft has been able to generate demand forecasts for various products while at the same time developing manufacturing, sourcing, and distributions plans.

The use of supply chain execution has also made it possible for the company to manage product flow starting from the initial stage up to the final stages. The availability of extranets courtesy of SCR also assists Microsoft to coordinate their various internal supply chain procedures since they can use extranets to coordinate various supply chain processes with other companies who are in partnership with them. SCR not only have extranets but also internet technology, and through the internet technology, Microsoft can facilitate global management of supply chain through provisions of connectivity for numerous organizations across the world. Various organizations have been in a position of sharing information all over the world courtesy of internet technology (Nettleton & Jensen 2007). Supply chain members can also enjoy improved communication amongst themselves and this improved communication helps in enhancing customer response, as well as various movements aimed at demand-driven models.

Customer Relationship Management System

Through the software, the company is able to provide rich capabilities that include modules for sales, services, and marketing together with analytical tools (Bill 2006). The software offers unique customization options that handle various operations of the company. Microsoft, being a big company, has several operations that cannot be handled without customization software and thus, the use of this software is beneficial to the company. Many customer-facing processes in marketing, sales, and customer services are achievable by the company due to integration and automation of the CRM. This has also enabled enterprise-wide customers' view since many processes are able to be concentrated on one given place through this process. Using CRM, Microsoft is able to track all its methods of interacting with customers and through the tracking; they are able to analyze the various customer responses for purposes of maximization of lifetime value for the customer (Nettleton & Jensen 2007). Integration and capturing of customer data is also possible using this process and Microsoft, and at the same time analyzing and distributing the results of the data to various customer touch points and customer-related systems. Provision of better services has been possible using these customer interactions and the ability to sell services and products that are new. The company uses CRM to identify non-profitable and profitable opportunities and customers.

Proper implementation of CRM systems has helped Microsoft to increase satisfaction for its various customers while reducing customer acquisition costs. Customer satisfaction is essential for this company in order to increase its sales volume, as well as to compete with its rival companies offering similar software products. Increase in sales revenues has been realized through the information from the CRM, and this has been possible through the identification of profitable consumers of their products. The company has a clear focus on segment market as well as cross-selling. Reduction of sales, marketing, and services is also possible through customer churn systems. The attainment in capabilities for operational and analytical CRM is possible using three CRM packages software. Microsoft uses these software, namely marketing, customer service, and sales for various integration processes.

E-Business Component of Microsoft

E-Business (Electronic Business) is information systems that support and drive business processes. E-business assists corporate organizations to connect external and internal business processes. It is the most revolutionary set of technology that has transformed businesses with a far reaching positive impact. E-Business does not only involve buying and selling on the internet, but also supporting customers, giving information about products and services, collaborating with other businesses, and advertising. Therefore, E-business is broader than commerce.

The core processes involved in e-business includes production process such as procurement, internal management processes such as organization, internal information sharing, customer-focused processes such as customer support, and advertisement and selling over the internet. Due to these cores processes, there exist different types of E-business known as e-commerce models: B2B (business-to-business) model involves processes that take place between organizations; C2C (consumer-to-consumer) refers to processes which involve individual consumers; and B2C (business-to-consumer) involves processes between consumers and company. B2G e-commerce involves processes that occur between companies and the public sector. Lastly, m-commerce involves businesses processes that are powered by mobile devices, especially smartphones. M-commerce has largely affected the telecommunication, retail, and financial industries (Bill 2006).

Microsoft has successfully used web technologies to successfully roll out its business services. From their website which powers all Microsoft's products and services, the B2C, C2C, and B2B models have been used. Microsoft promotes their products and services by offering rich and interactive information on their sites. All products that belong to Microsoft are found on their site. By offering information on the internet which is a public infrastructure, there is enormous saving in costs. Since information is posted on the websites as soon as it happens, it reduces the cycle time and thus offers timely information. There is also better customer service offered by the website to its customer. Customers ask questions and timely answers are provided by support. In fact, Microsoft's site offers 24-hour support, 365 days a year. Relationship between Microsoft also improves because questions and suggestions asked by customers are recorded and are used to improve products and services every day. Use of the web allows Microsoft customers to customize products; for example, when downloading certain products such as an SQL server, one can choose the product version as well as services that are offered by the same product. Besides, many customers can download the same copy of product software from any part of the world. In addition, there is increased convenience of doing business using the site (Bill 2006). For example, there is no limit of doing business in terms of location and time, and information on products and services reaches customers and other business in real time. For Microsoft, their website offers an infinite store for information from their customers, as well as infinite shelf for its products and services.

From the benefits that have been identified, Microsoft has used different benefit models to meet their needs. Summarily, Microsoft has used its website for customer support, advertising, market awareness, sales, and electronic information services. The sales benefit exists because when customers download a trial version of the software, they have an option to buy and pay for a product key on the internet. User can also buy any product straight without using trial versions. Therefore, Microsoft reduces costs because there is no burden of distributing their products physically. For Microsoft, the web offers informational or communicational and transactional strategies by supplementing traditional marketing and building a virtual business.

Microsoft's website satisfies the B2C e-commerce model as most information on the websites and the support is directed to the customers. Since most products developed by Microsoft are used by other businesses, there is much information which guides other enterprises on product use and any partnership available with Microsoft. Therefore, the website satisfies the B2B model. For example, the site gives information relevant to HP, SAP, and Hortworks. When customers post information on the site, other customers are able to see it. This brings about the C2C model.

All the benefits discussed from above, together with the models that Microsoft websites satisfies, is due to the cutting edge design of the website.

The website's home page (http://www.microsoft.com/en-us/default.aspx) has all the information covering Microsoft's products and services. All the products that Microsoft deals with are listed with links. There are also graphics to ensure that there is quick recognition and recall. The upper navigation provides an easy way of getting to other areas of the website. The central part of the websites provides sufficient space for showcasing new products and services.

The website has a search feature which consists of a simple input textbox and appears in every page of the site. This enables visitors to quickly search anything on the site such as information about products, services, events, announcements, and even posts from customers (Lehman, Lehman & Feazell 2011). On the site, the Download link gives customers a way of downloading software from the site. This includes trial versions and free software like utilities. The same copy can be downloaded by many users across the globe. The site also allows the user to buy products via the Shop link. Users are able to see the features of the product and the price among other information. The most remarkable thing is that users can pay electronically. Through the Products link, the site offers information and documentation of all the products made by Microsoft. Both new products and existing ones are available. Services are also listed, and each has a link for more information. Through the support link, the website offers information that supports users on the use of Microsoft products. In fact, the support is categorized by resource, type of user, product, and topic. This makes it easier to get information. Still on support, each item of concern enables a user to submit views on how important the support offered was. The support also enables a user to create an account which enables one to get help or receive email notifications on events and new products. Users can subscribe to RSS feeds and newsletters as well (Lehman, Lehman & Feazell 2011). The site has done much to satisfy a number of concerns relating to E-business. However, due to the rate of growth of Microsoft, the following improvements would help:

- Microsoft has many products which, when in one website, make it hard to find information. Instead of using sub domains, independent sites should be created for each website.
- Microsoft's current C2C model is not efficient. Therefore, a blog is necessary to allow customers to discuss personal experiences on different products.

Knowledge Management

Microsoft has for a long time used successful knowledge management (KM) to continuously and consistently make intelligent decisions regarding information systems. The modern and stiff antagonism in the market brings about the aspect of market battles in terms of costs associated with manufacturing and the addition of customer value to the systems. Knowledge management is therefore significant in the storage, allotment, and usage of information with the intention of refining the knowledge throughout the cycle of management business asset that prevents Microsoft from spending time reinventing solutions, as well as maintain organizational focus on providing high quality outputs (Lehman, Lehman & Feazell 2011).

One of the main roles that knowledge management has played in Microsoft organization is to refine information and stimulate variant actions. In the effective employment of knowledge management tools, Microsoft had to differentiate between data, information, and knowledge as data was raw and involved unprocessed observations. Through this, the company was able to understand both the negative and positive stock chart signals, providing an effective notice to the investors of the company to exit losing positions. It is therefore evident that knowledge has both humanistic and scientific roots which can be created, shared, applied, and tested as long as we are able to communicate.

The second role that knowledge management has played is to facilitate the classification, understanding, and control of norms and standards within the organization. Substantive norms are in place to define organizational strategy, communicative customs define pathways of notification, and control customs define how to appraise the task execution specified. When these norms are applied to the processes of management, they can aid in the codification of basic knowledge related to the processes and systems efficiently. This elementary codification ensures accountability (Lehman, Lehman & Feazell 2011). Microsoft company ensures that the resolve of this codification and breakdown is to examine which processes support the organization's competencies, and reinforce those proficiencies by making them routine. Knowledge management is much expansive than this application, but it is beneficial for recognizing and even altering organizational culture and basic norms.

The third role that knowledge management has offered Microsoft is to track employee feedback and assert whether the person is responsive, thus increasing the probability that the user will successfully internalize the knowledge provided (Arnold 2011). Most of the affective domains characterize how employees react to information to different types of information provided. At the lowest level, employees must take the information in a while at the highest level; a knowledge management system might track a person's feedback and be able to assert his or her responsiveness, thus increasing the chance that he or she will successfully internalize the information. In most cases, the employees are classified in the cognitive section by knowing, understanding, applying, and analyzing the object knowledge, thereby making them fairly experts. On the other hand, employees who additionally synthesize and evaluate the same knowledge object would therefore be the better alternative to turn to for learning and transfer of knowledge. Despite this domain being the least used by knowledge management systems, Microsoft ensures that the manufacturing procedures are often modified by experts in the technical area to effectively gain optimal results.

With the benefit of helping the Microsoft Company to become a knowledge-potential firm, the knowledge management mechanisms have been of significance to the company. The first benefit is that they have initiated and enabled the company to outline high-level goals and provide different strategies in an effort to achieve them. Secondly, the knowledge management systems have enabled identification of real needs as well as issues which occur in the Company, thereby offering a framework for eliminating them. Despite being a new strategy to the company, the knowledge management systems were in place to illustrate effectively the type of business that Microsoft Company was running, the business needs required, as well as the budget provided. This was a beneficial to the company as it enabled the company to choose the right programs which suited it effectively (Arnold 2011).

Global Information Management

Information systems have provided numerous benefits to the Microsoft Company from analysis of collected raw data, to production of quality output. Despite these benefits, the organization has had to deal and manage global aspects in regard to the information systems including the challenges faced, technologies used, and strategic advantages gained. Microsoft constantly collects information on their vendors, customers, and competitors to make strategies and make strategic decisions that enable the company to compete effectively. Most of the information used to do this is called business intelligence and it relies heavily on the data quality. The four main elements used to measure the quality of business intelligence include timeliness, accessibility, form, and validity. The use of this kind of information to make decisions outside the necessary time parameters has consistently affected its quality of timeliness. To limit this, Microsoft puts polices and guidelines to deny managers access to the internal databases holding critical information.

The first global challenge that the information systems in Microsoft faced included managerial literacy whereby the manager's knowledge in both technology and information is imperative to establish how effective strategies will be when put in place. A technology-literate leader will mostly know how and when to apply technology (Arnold 2011). This therefore means that he will know what to buy to execute specific processes and the most proper time to make the purchase or implement a specific program. An information-literate manager is also able to define what information is required and how to access it effectively and efficiently. He poses the ability to convert it from information to business intelligence, as well as to make the best decisions based on the information provided or collected.

The second challenge is security whereby crucial information may be removed from the systems of the company. Microsoft ensured that they built safeguards to restrict access to the database, disallowing the modification and manipulation of data by unauthorized users. The company also ensured that they provided adequate protection against virus or malware attacks.

Loss of data is damaging to any organization, thereby making backup and recovery an integral challenge in information systems. Microsoft ensured that the systems incorporated in the software features regular backup. This is done so that management will be adequately protected against system failure or sabotage. In case of system failure, restoration of transactions, balances, and statements from the data backed up by the company is possible.

Fault tolerance proves to be another global challenge faced by the information systems as they should be tolerant to the variant natural and human glitches like unreliable power supply occurrences during the course of operations. The Microsoft Company ensured that systems will continue to function normally and will continuously notify the management of such failures. In incidences of total failure, the system was able to restart accurately.

Handling of data has been a crucial factor for Microsoft during the end processing period. It has therefore developed software that is capable of accurately manipulating data as instructed. Human workload has been significantly reduced as it relates data of up to one whole financial year automatically (Arnold 2011).

The company has to be readily available and accessible to its users, especially during its peak hours when all its systems are in use. It has also been able to handle its infrastructural services well. Software upgrades is necessary for the company to add new functionalities to the existing systems. Version upgrade in time has been significant in managing the high costs of service. As the company grows, it has had to change its MIS software as it serves as an important factor in the handling of its major operations (El Shazly & Butts 2002).

References

Bill, B 2006, What's new at Microsoft? *DM Review*, vol. 16, no. 11, pp. 50-52.

Nettleton, E & Jensen, W 2007, 'Microsoft stops McDonald serving spam', *Journal of Database Marketing & Customer Strategy Management*, vol. 14, no. 3, pp. 254-257.

El Shazly, MR & Butts, RJ 2002, 'In quest of profits: legal and ethical implications facing Microsoft', *International Journal of Social Economics*, vol. 29, no. 5, pp. 346-355.

Lehman, MW, Lehman, CM & Feazell, J 2011, 'Dashboard your scorecard: unleash the power of Excel for visual data analysis', *Journal of Accountancy*, vol. 211, no. 2, pp. 20-27.

Arnold, SE 2011, 'Microsoft escalates the war on the multidevice user experience', *Information Today*, vol. 28, no. 8, pp. 18-19.